THEN *&* NOW

DES MOINES

OPPOSITE: The Iowa State Capitol glows in this nighttime image from the 1980s. (Courtesy Iowa Department of Transportation.)

THEN & NOW

DES MOINES

Craig S. McCue

For my family—my inspiration, my life

Published by Arcadia Publishing
Charleston, South Carolina

Printed in the United States of America

Then and Now is a registered trademark and is used under license from
Salamander Books Limited

For all general information, please contact Arcadia Publishing:
Telephone 843-853-2070
Fax 843-853-0044
E-mail sales@arcadiapublishing.com
For customer service and orders:
Toll-Free 1-888-313-2665

Visit us on the Internet at www.arcadiapublishing.com

ON THE FRONT COVER: John Vachon worked for the Farm Security Administration documenting the conditions of the rural poor in America, eventually becoming a staff photographer for *Life* and *Look* magazines. He took this photograph of the Iowa State Capitol looking down Locust Street in 1940 as part of a series on rural life. (Then, courtesy Library of Congress; Now, courtesy the author.)

ON THE BACK COVER: Zoo Lake was the location of the Des Moines Zoological Gardens, which later became the site of Riverview Amusement Park. (Courtesy Ron Playle.)

CONTENTS

ACKNOWLEDGMENTS

I want to thank first of all the people who are working to preserve history and make it available to everyone: Pat Meiners, Sarah Oltrogge, Natasha Moore, and the other members of the Des Moines Historical Society who share their photographs and artifacts on their Facebook group; Kent Carlson, Mark Heggen, and the other members of the "Lost Des Moines" Facebook group; Bill Sherman, Peggy Jester, Elaine Estes, and the other members of the Polk County Historical Society; and the members of the West Des Moines Historical Society.

A very special thank-you goes to Thomas Wenck and Archie and Ryan Cook, who went through the manuscript with a fine-tooth comb. I appreciate all of your help in bringing this project together.

I also want to thank the libraries and individuals who made their collections available for this work: the photograph archives of the Iowa Department of Transportation, the photograph archives of the Des Moines Public Library, the Memory Archives of the Library of Congress, and the postcard collection of Ron Playle. Special thanks go to contributors Burgess Shields, Ethel Reames, Michael Magee, and others who donated personal collections for historical preservation.

All of the Then photographs in this book came from these archives, or from the author's own collection of antiquarian books, many of which contained historic photographs of Des Moines now in the public domain. The references I have used for photographs and research include:

Brigham, Johnson. *History of Des Moines and Polk County*. Chicago: S.J. Clarke,1911.

————. *Iowa, Its History and Its Foremost Citizens*. Chicago: S.J. Clarke, 1918.

Denny, Robert. *Sesquicentennial Salute to Des Moines and the State of Iowa*. n.p.: Educators Press, 1993.

Des Moines City Council. *Second Annual Report of the City of Des Moines* (1909), *Sixth Annual Report of the City of Des Moines* (1913), *Ninth Annual Report of the City of Des Moines* (1916). Private collection.

Dixon, J.M. *Centennial History of Polk County, Iowa*. Des Moines: State Register, 1876.

Hunt, Enos B. Jr. *Des Moines Beautiful*. Des Moines: self-published,1910.

Hussey, Tacitus. *Beginnings: Reminiscences of Early Des Moines*. Des Moines: American Lithograph, 1919.

Porter, Will. *Annals of Polk County, Iowa, and city of Des Moines*. Des Moines: Geo. A. Miller, 1898.

Pratt, LeRoy G. *From Cabin to Capital City: A Brief History of Des Moines and Polk County, Iowa*. Johnston, IA: Heartland Area Education Agency, 1990.

Wilcox, Charles. *Des Moines Illustrated Souvenir*. Des Moines: Historical Illustrative Co., 1895.

Most of the Now photographs were taken by the author, and a few were taken from the archives listed above.

INTRODUCTION

I have always enjoyed reading about history. Not necessarily modern reinterpretations—I like to read old books and magazines that show us history as it was being made: articles in *Harper's Weekly* about the progress of the Civil War, *Life* pictorials on World War II as it happened, pioneer journals describing the hopes, struggles, and achievements of those settlers, even as they occurred. I also enjoy old histories of Des Moines, written by J.M. Dixon, Johnson Brigham, and Tacitus Hussey, who not only took the time to document what came before, but also what was happening in their own era.

But of all the different kinds of history books available, I think I like Then & Now books the most. It is one thing to read contemporary accounts, but to see history in photographs, as it occurred, and then be able to see what has changed since then, adds a new dimension to the experience. In comparing old and new, I wonder: Why did this building survive, and this other one get torn down? Why did this elegant home become a hovel? What motivation was behind the removal or realignment of a street? How did an area slowly shift from upscale residential to commercial and retail? Did change occur through happenstance, or was there a plan? And how were the people transformed, as they lived their lives through those changing times?

Des Moines has seen much in the way of transformation over its history. Starting out as a frontier garrison, it provided a waypoint and provisioning stop for pioneers headed west. It mustered troops to defend liberty during the Civil War, and honored them when they returned. Railroads linked the city to the nation, and Des Moines thanked them with the large coal reserves it held. Business and commerce began to thrive, even as the city hosted not only the state capitol, but other local, state, and federal government services as well.

Coal brought electricity and smog. The former allowed the trolley system to be electrified in 1888—only the second city in America to do so at the time. The latter resulted in demands for more beautiful spaces for citizens to enjoy. Together, these influences fed a demand for expansion, and in 1890 the city annexed several suburbs, growing larger than Boston or San Francisco in the process. On the heels of this expansion, the City Beautiful movement was born, and one of the group's first acts was to petition for six separate parks be set aside in the newly annexed areas. Other parks, offering bandstands, rides, and other amusements, sprang up at the ends of trolley lines to encourage ridership on the weekends.

New neighborhoods were plotted and built, and the trolleys rolled through them to newly established cities such as Valley Junction and Urbandale. Colleges like Highland Park, Des Moines College, Grandview, and Drake University also set up their campuses along these lines, and Des Moines became a center of higher education. Industrial pioneers set up shop, with leaders such as Mason and the Duesenberg brothers building some of the earliest automobiles.

Another movement in the city was the Des Moines Plan, a reaction to the perceived political corruption at city hall at the time. Cronyism and backroom deals resulted in a progressive backlash, and a new form of commission government was proposed and formally introduced in 1907. It proved to be hugely successful and an example to the nation.

With the new organization, the streets were finally paved, fire and police service became standardized, and a new civic center was built along the riverfront. Businessmen in the city installed electrical lighting in the downtown area, paid for out of their own profits.

The blossoming of new public works brought national attention, and funds were provided to build Fort Des Moines and Camp Dodge. Both bases were instrumental during World War I—the 17th Provisional Training Regiment, for "colored" officers, was based out of Fort Des Moines; while Camp Dodge trained more than 100,000 troops for the war effort. During World War II, the stables and cavalry barracks were converted for the first Women's Army Corps (WAC) training center.

In many ways, the early years of the 20th century were Des Moines' golden era. The pioneers of that day had a vision for the future and gave their utmost to see it come to pass. But progress is inevitable, and sometimes history gets in the way. A shining civic center dulls with age. Homes of pioneers decay and are torn down or converted to lower-income housing. Architectural marvels are sacrificed for expediency, demolished when upgrades to bring them to code would cost more than the building is worth. Other classic structures are torn down to provide parking for retail outlets in the downtown area—which, in turn, move out to the suburbs a few years later with the opening of the first malls. New buildings replace old, and the city shifts to follow the patterns laid out by the next generation.

The problem is, there is not a lot of history left to preserve. So as you read this book, I would like to ask a favor: I would like you to think about the history still around you. Is there something—an old heirloom, a picture, a locale that brings back memories? Is it worth preserving for the next generation? If you do find an opportunity to save some of the old, then, please, take advantage of it while you can.

I would also like you to pause every once in awhile to consider the pioneers' story. Experience with your own eyes what they built, and what it meant for their community. And I would like you to ask yourself: do I have a vision? Is there something of the pioneer spirit in me? If so, then I hope you consider taking a risk. Become a pioneer for the next generation, and step out to see that vision become a reality.

CHAPTER

POSTCARDS FROM
ANOTHER TIME

In the early 1900s, Des Moines residents worked together to establish businesses, colleges, infrastructure, and civic buildings—all to better their society. Shown clockwise from the upper left are Union Station, the Sixth Street Bridge, the Federal Courthouse, Highland Park College, and the Iowa State Capitol, the only building which survived. (Courtesy Ron Playle.)

The last cabin of the old Fort Des Moines survived into the 20th century, but not much longer. For many years, a park marked the birthplace of the city near the junction of the Des Moines and Raccoon Rivers. In 1964, the Polk County Historical Society had another cabin from Washington County, also built in the 1840s, moved to the spot. Recently, an expansion of the Martin Luther King Jr. Parkway threatened the cabin, but the city was able to route the road around it. (From *Iowa, Its History and Its Foremost Citizens*.)

Though Des Moines was designated as the capital of Iowa in 1857, construction on a permanent capitol building would not begin until 1871. It was paid for through subscription, allowing the structure to be completed without any debt but delaying completion until 1886. The Iowa General Assembly moved from the old brick capitol at the site of the Soldiers and Sailors Monument in 1884, while the dome was still being completed. (Courtesy Des Moines Public Library.)

POSTCARDS FROM ANOTHER TIME

In 1904, a worker's lamp started a fire in the attic of the Iowa State Capitol, above the Iowa House of Representatives' chamber (seen here around 1890). The fire crashed through the ceiling, covering the floor with debris. While firefighters fought the blaze from the north, volunteers rescued the Civil War battle flags and the volumes of the law library, using improvised chutes to carry the books away. After the fire was extinguished, representatives continued to meet in the chamber during repairs, even though the damage was extensive. (From *Des Moines Illustrated Souvenir*.)

POSTCARDS FROM ANOTHER TIME

The Iowa Supreme Court chamber, located beneath the house of representatives' chamber, suffered severe water damage from the firefighting efforts. All of the frescoes seen here were destroyed, though most of the hanging art was saved. The restoration effort included repairing the damaged wing, as well as adding electric lighting, elevators, and telephones to the building. New artwork was also commissioned from the many Iowa residents who wanted to help. Now that the Iowa Supreme Court meets in its own building, this room is used for conferences. (From *Des Moines Illustrated Souvenir*.)

The first federal building in Des Moines was authorized by Congress in 1865. A site adjacent to the Polk County Courthouse at Court Avenue and Fifth Street was selected, and final construction was completed in 1871. In 1890, it was expanded with a fourth floor and tower. The building originally housed the post office, federal courtrooms, and tax and land offices, though many of these functions would eventually move elsewhere. (Then, courtesy the author; Now, courtesy Library of Congress.)

The Equitable Life Assurance Company built its headquarters in 1891 at the northwest corner of Sixth Avenue and Locust Street, adding four more floors in 1911. When Equitable built its new headquarters across the street in 1924, this building was purchased by Banker's Trust. Ruan Corporation acquired the Banker's Trust company and built its tower next to the historic building in 1975. (Then, from *Des Moines Illustrated Souvenir*; Now, courtesy Library of Congress.)

In this view of Sixth Avenue facing south at Locust Street, the heart of Des Moines' financial district during the city's golden era is shown, providing access to both commercial and retail enterprises. Both intercity trolleys and interurban electrics could access the hub, making it a busy and profitable intersection. The tall structure to the right is the Fleming Building, still standing just behind the new Equitable Building today. (From *History of Des Moines and Polk County*.)

Looking east down Locust Street at Sixth Avenue, the Observatory Building, since replaced by the Capital Square complex, is visible. On the left are the Alexandria, Family, and Casino Theaters and the Franklin Hotel. The clock in the foreground belongs to Josephs Jewelers, still in operation. The only building still standing in this view is the Iowa State Capitol far in the distance. (From *History of Des Moines and Polk County*.)

Across from the Observatory Building/Capital Square is the Savery Hotel—now Renaissance Savery. It was established in 1886 by a group of businessmen who named it after the first Savery Hotel that later became the Kirkwood. Even though it offered luxurious accommodations, the building proved to be too expensive to modernize and was rebuilt from scratch in 1919 on the same site. (Courtesy Ron Playle.)

This view of the financial district around 1910 shows Grand Avenue between Second Avenue and Third Street. It was featured as a popular postcard of the time and illustrates the heavy smog layer that circulated in Des Moines because of the coal-fired power providing electricity to the city. Though the Observatory Building and Savery Hotel can be clearly seen, the old Equitable Building, just three blocks down, is nothing but a haze. (From *Des Moines Beautiful.*)

The original Savery Hotel, built in 1856, was located on Walnut and Fourth Streets. It was extensively refurbished and renamed the Kirkwood, after one of Iowa's most popular governors, Samuel J. Kirkwood, in 1878. The building caught fire on April 6, 1929, and was demolished to make way for a new, more modern hotel. The facility recently went through a conversion to executive apartments. (Courtesy Ron Playle.)

POSTCARDS FROM ANOTHER TIME

Walnut Street, seen from Eighth Street, was the heart of the retail sector in Des Moines for many years. The anchor store was Younkers, on the left, which remained in the downtown area until 2005. On the far right is the Foster Building, once home to a popular opera house. In the distance are the more recent Hub Tower and EMC Insurance Building. (Courtesy Ron Playle.)

This is actually the third county courthouse in Des Moines, built in 1906 to replace a much smaller structure serving as courthouse and jail. It originally opened with four courtrooms; the facility now holds 28 separate courts, with overflow moved to other, leased facilities. Discussions are underway for temporary and permanent resolution of the overcrowded court system. (Courtesy Des Moines Public Library.)

Court Avenue marked the southern boundary of the financial district. It was also the main point of entry for most rail traffic because the Rock Island and Union stations were both next to the courthouse. With revitalization efforts currently underway, the street has become the center of nightlife in the downtown area, hosting upscale restaurants and other venues for young residents living in the newly built condominiums lining the district. (From *History of Des Moines and Polk County*.)

This view down Locust Street features the Crocker and Observatory Buildings on the right, with the Savery Hotel on the left side of the street and the Iowa State Capitol in the distance. The Now image showcases the tops of the EMC Insurance Building, the Financial Center, Hub Tower, and the Equitable Building, with the Register and Tribune Building on the left and the Capital Square and Iowa State Capitol in the distance. Though they are a necessity, many local residents resent the sparse and unremarkable parking garages interspersed throughout downtown. (Courtesy Ron Playle.)

POSTCARDS FROM ANOTHER TIME

The northern sections of Des Moines were mostly industrial along the riverfront, where coal-fired electrical plants provided much-needed energy for the city. The coal mines dotting the Des Moines metro area, which provided the coal used in these plants, have long since ceased operation. In the Now image, the Des Moines River is crossed by University Avenue, Interstate 235, and the arch-covered Center Street Bridge for pedestrians and bicyclists, which crosses the river at the dam. Residential condominiums and parks have replaced the industrial plants of the past. On the far left is the new Wells Fargo Arena. (Courtesy the author.)

POSTCARDS FROM ANOTHER TIME

Drake University was founded by Dr. George Carpenter in 1881. He brought with him most of the students and almost the entire faculty of Oskaloosa College, a struggling school founded by the Disciples of Christ. Gen. Francis Marion Drake, Dr. Carpenter's brother-in-law, sponsored much of the early development of the campus, funded through his personal fortune. Old Main still serves as the administrative center of the university. (From *Des Moines Beautiful*.)

Grand View College was founded in 1895 as a school and seminary for the Danish Lutheran Church. Though small, it steadily continued to enroll students, mostly Danish, for ministerial and professional education. In 1975, the college began its first four-year program of study. Now a university, it recently established an MS program for Innovative Leadership. (Courtesy Ron Playle.)

The Urban Parks Movement in Des Moines came on the heels of a much larger conservation movement in the late 19th century. The first purchase made by the city, in 1894, was for 60 acres east and north of Thompson's Bend, now known as Union Park. The Floral Gardens rotunda was completely rebuilt for the Heritage Carousel, which still offers rides during the summer season. (From *Des Moines Annual Reports*.)

The first cement bridge in the city was constructed along Locust Street in 1909, after the flood of 1903 severely damaged most of the existing bridges crossing the Des Moines and Raccoon Rivers. It has survived several inundations since then, including the disastrous flood of 1993, though its facade and railings have been redone. Next to the bridge is the old public library building, now the home of the World Food Prize. (From *Des Moines Beautiful*.)

Jefferson S. Polk was one of the organizers, along with Hoyt Sherman and Fred Hubbell, of the Equitable Life Insurance Company. He also served as the president of the Des Moines City Railway Company, among other ventures, and lived at Herndon Hall, at 2000 Grand Avenue. Built in 1883, it is now known as the Bergman Mansion, one of the few Victorian homes left along Grand Avenue, and serves as a doctor's office. (From *Des Moines Beautiful*.)

Terrace Hill at 2300 Grand Avenue was built in the Second Empire style by B.F. Allen in 1869 at a cost of $250,000. Spectaculars were held at the house, drawing people from as far away as Chicago and St. Louis. It was purchased by Fred M. Hubbell in 1884 and used as the family residence until it was donated to the state in 1971 to be used specifically as the Iowa Governor's Mansion. (From *Des Moines Beautiful.*)

Because of cheap coal-fired power plants, electricity drove the expansion of the city, from electric trolleys to factories and commercial ventures. Walnut Street was the first to have electric lighting installed, in 1906. Illuminated by Tungsten Electroliers, it was pronounced by *Electrical World* as "The Best Lighted Street in the United States." Now, the Capital Square and the Kirkwood dominate this same intersection at Fourth Street. (From *Des Moines Annual Reports*.)

Soon, other streets in the downtown area were lit, with the entire cost born by the business community of Des Moines. This view of Locust Street facing east from Seventh Street shows the Chamberlain Hotel (now Banker's Trust), the many theaters of the era, including the Alexandria and the Unique, and on the right the Flynn Building, built in 1885 and still standing. (From *Des Moines Annual Reports*.)

This 1910 view of downtown from the Iowa State Capitol shows much of the newly created civic center along the riverfront, including the post office, library, Coliseum, and Municipal Building. Farther down Locust Street are the two tallest structures in the downtown area, the Observatory and Old Equitable Buildings. Now, the city features 15 separate downtown buildings taller than the Polk County Courthouse, which tops out at 160 feet. (From *Des Moines Annual Reports*.)

POSTCARDS FROM ANOTHER TIME

CHAPTER 2

GONE BUT NOT FORGOTTEN

The John MacVicar Freeway, designated as Interstate 235, was built in the early 1960s, with construction starting between Keo Way and the Des Moines River. It would eventually link both Interstate 80 and Interstate 35, making Des Moines the "Crossroads of the Nation." Unfortunately, the freeway had to cut across some of the oldest neighborhoods in the city, demolishing many historical landmarks in the process. (Courtesy Iowa Department of Transportation.)

The old Federal Building continued to serve, even as the post office and the federal courthouses moved elsewhere. Many fought for preservation, but the building needed significant repairs, and it was finally demolished in 1968. The main reason for its removal was the fact that downtown outlets were threatening to move unless additional parking were added. (Courtesy the author.)

Equitable Life Insurance moved to its new building when it was completed in 1924. The company's old headquarters was sold to Banker's Trust, which used it even after it was purchased by the Ruan Corporation. When the 36-floor Ruan Tower was completed in 1975, the Banker's Trust offices were moved to that location. Preservationists fought to preserve and restore the building, but Ruan could not find tenants willing to pay for its upgrade, and it was torn down in 1980 to make way for the Ruan 2 office complex. (Courtesy Ron Playle.)

The Coliseum was constructed in 1908 and served for many years as a center for sporting events and conventions. Though it was supposedly fireproof, the building caught fire August 13, 1949, and had to be demolished. Planning immediately began for the new sports complex at Veterans Memorial Auditorium. The site is now home to the Riverfront YMCA, which provides supportive housing in addition to recreational facilities. (Courtesy the author.)

Coliseum Building, Des Moines, Iowa.

GONE BUT NOT FORGOTTEN

Webster and Alcott Schools, on Lyon Street between East Twelfth and Thirteenth Streets, provided primary education to boys and girls, though separately for a time. The schools were in the East Des Moines School District, which operated autonomously until 1907. Founded in 1874, the schools lasted until 1963, when they were closed because of freeway construction. The location now serves as parking for Mercy Medical Center. (Courtesy Des Moines Public Library.)

Originally planned to be four
stories in 1903, the Chamberlain
Hotel grew to six stories before
its completion in 1911. D.S.
Chamberlain hired W.L. Brown,
the former manager of the Savery
Hotel, to oversee construction of
the building. It was demolished in
1975 to make way for the Ruan
Center. The location is now home to
a Banker's Trust branch office. (From
Des Moines Beautiful.)

GONE BUT NOT FORGOTTEN

Located at 601 Sixth Avenue, the Victoria Hotel was built in 1899 in a European style at a cost of $50,000, on the site of the former residence of Dr. Francis Grimmel, a pioneer physician and community leader. It expanded in 1910, although at the time community leaders did not believe Des Moines required that much hotel space. Currently, the site is a parking lot for the American Republic Insurance Company. (Courtesy Ron Playle.)

17 Victoria Hotel, Des Moines, Iowa

In this view of Fourth Street facing north, between Locust and Walnut Streets, the Princess Theatre is on the right, the edge of the Observatory Building on the left, and in the distance is the old YMCA. This entire block—and even the street itself—was demolished to make way for the Capital Square building and Nollen Plaza. (Courtesy Iowa Department of Transportation.)

Even with the demolition of the Observatory Building in 1937, the intersection continued to be a bustling transportation corridor into the 1950s. The area declined in the 1970s and was slated for urban renewal. The only building to survive in this view was the Savery Hotel. Construction on the Capital Square building and adjacent Nollen Plaza—sometimes called the umbrella park because of the large sculpture, *Crusoe Umbrella*, located in the northeast corner—was completed in 1984. (Courtesy Library of Congress.)

Des Moines College was founded in 1864 as a Baptist school and seminary. It moved to this new campus on College Avenue and Ninth Street in 1884. Suffering financial difficulties, the college merged with Central College and Highland Park College to become Des Moines University. The location is now a park located next to the old Dowling High School and the Department of Corrections office complex. (Courtesy Des Moines Public Library.)

GONE BUT NOT FORGOTTEN

Highland Park College, originally built in 1889 by a group of businessmen, became the campus of the old Des Moines University in 1918. The school was forced to close in 1929 after a takeover by a fundamentalist group led to riots and the mass departure of most of the faculty. Alfred Lawson purchased the property in 1943 for his School of Lawsonomy but it closed in 1954. The site is now the location of the Park Fair Mall. The current Des Moines University was originally the Still College of Osteopathic Medicine, founded in 1898. (Courtesy Des Moines Public Library.)

The Van Ginkel Building at Fourth and Locust Streets was built in 1895 as Des Moines's first skyscraper, later known as the Observatory Building because of the view from its five-story tower. Many residents feared the height of the structure would prevent firefighters from stopping a blaze. It had trouble retaining tenants and was eventually torn down in 1937. The site is now home to the Capital Square Mall. (Courtesy the author.)

Observatory Building, Des Moines, Iowa.

This building was originally known as the Turner Block, then as the Crocker Building. Located on the southwest corner of Seventh Street and Sycamore Street (now Grand Avenue), it was first occupied by the Studebaker Carriage Company. After a significant expansion, it then served as the home of the Des Moines Life Insurance Company (later Union Life) for many years. Marriott built a 33-story downtown hotel and convention center on the site in 1981. (From *Des Moines Beautiful.*)

Sedgewick Brinsmaid built his home in 1901 at Thirty-sixth Street and Grand Avenue. It was the first Prairie School structure in Iowa. Brinsmaid, a glass merchant, included many Art Deco stained-glass pieces in his home, which had no parallel in the country. The house was demolished in 1971 to make way for condominiums centered around retirement living. In 1978, 3660 Grand Avenue was completed. (Courtesy Library of Congress.)

GONE BUT NOT FORGOTTEN

Edwin Thomas Meredith became general manager of his family's publishing business in 1896. In 1902, he began publishing the periodical *Successful Farming*, and followed that in 1922 with the magazine that would eventually become *Better Homes and Gardens*. He lived in this house at Forty-second Street and Ingersoll Avenue, now the site of the Plymouth Place retirement and assisted living facility. (From *Des Moines Beautiful*.)

Though urban renewal has its benefits, one side effect is the removal of historic buildings. Such was the case with the 500 block of East Locust Street, where almost every building was torn down and replaced. Frequently, older buildings simply are not rentable or are too cost-prohibitive to upgrade to modern standards. In this case, obsolete retail and office space was converted to lofts and condominiums, with smaller storefronts and garages on the first floor. (Courtesy Library of Congress.)

GONE BUT NOT FORGOTTEN

These duplexes along Nineteenth Street just north of Grand Avenue were among the first attempts at high-occupancy residential living along the highly popular residential corridor. As more and more people moved to the area, stately homes were torn down to make way for apartment blocks and high-rise condominiums. Today, the space provides parking for the television station across the street and for the Finkbine Mansion, which survives as a corporate office. (From *Des Moines Beautiful*.)

This home was built for Genevieve den Hartog at 2210 Army Post Road in 1940 in the Moderne Art Deco style. It was positioned to allow easy viewing of airplanes taking off from the Des Moines airport. Though attempts were made to place it in the historic register, it lay in the path of runway expansion. Because the home was built of waylight block and cement, it could not be moved and was torn down in the late 1980s. (Courtesy Library of Congress.)

Des Moines needed to route traffic around the city hub, and the Martin Luther King Jr. Parkway was proposed. The western portion of that route was the former Twentieth Street, which required the removal of most of the homes and businesses along that road. Construction continues on the parkway, and a bridge across the Des Moines River was recently completed. The road stretches as far as East Sixth Street and will eventually reach US Highway 65. (Courtesy Library of Congress.)

School Street was named for the several primary and secondary schools lining it, schools that had broad spaces useful for conversion to freeway routes. On this particular section of Interstate 235 near Nineteenth Street, it also required the excavation of a deep trench through the oldest parts of the city. It was a loss felt by many, and as a result, historic districts such as Sherman Hill have now been set up to preserve historical homes and businesses. (Courtesy Iowa Department of Transportation.)

Construction significantly changed the dynamic of many neighborhoods near the freeway. Urban decay began to settle in, and this once fine home at 1059 Ninth Street was eventually converted to low-income apartments. In the 1970s and 1980s, urban renewal projects were sponsored to correct the problem. This home was removed as part of the Walnut Hill Redevelopment Project in 1981; the property ultimately became part of the urban campus of Des Moines Area Community College. (Courtesy Library of Congress.)

Soldiers and sailors on leave line up to see the movie *Bataan* in 1943. The Des Moines and adjacent Paramount Theaters featured popular movies in the downtown area, such as *State Fair*, which opened nationally in 1945 at both theaters. The Des Moines Theater was torn down in 1969, and the Paramount 10 years later. The Polk County Convention Center was built on the property in 1985. (Courtesy West Des Moines Historical Society.)

GONE BUT NOT FORGOTTEN

Riverview Amusement Park opened in 1915 at the site of the Des Moines Zoological Gardens and featured many popular rides and attractions. While kids enjoyed the rides, teens and adults enjoyed dancing and music at the Riviera Ballroom. The park continued until 1979, when Adventureland purchased the park and relocated most of the rides to Altoona. Discussions were underway on finding a use for the ballroom itself until the building caught fire (some suspected arson) and burned to the ground in 1981. (Courtesy Ron Playle.)

N-442 RIVIERA BALLROOM & FREE PLAYGROUNDS RIVERVIEW PARK DES MOINES, IOWA

The Sixth Avenue Melan Arch Bridge was hailed as an example of modern infrastructure development by the city when it was completed in 1907. It stood until 1965, when, after several weeks of heavy flooding, the center span of the bridge collapsed. No one was injured, though telephone service north of the city was lost. As part of the restoration after the flood, new bridges were completed for Sixth Avenue, University Avenue, Walnut Street, and the Seventh Street viaduct. All were reopened in 1966. (From *Des Moines Annual Reports*.)

GONE BUT NOT FORGOTTEN

CHAPTER

THE JOURNEY
TO NOW

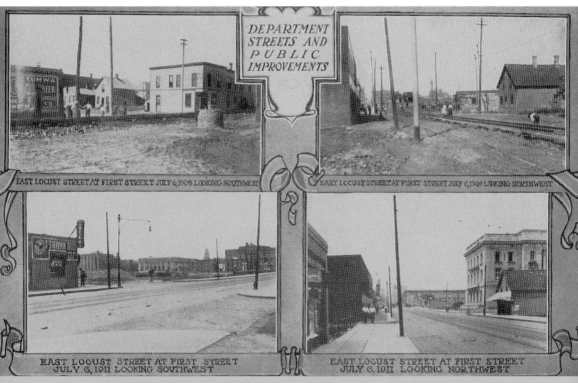

EAST LOCUST STREET AT FIRST STREET JULY 6, 1909 LOOKING SOUTHWEST

EAST LOCUST STREET AT FIRST STREET JULY 6, 1909 LOOKING NORTHWEST

EAST LOCUST STREET AT FIRST STREET JULY 6, 1911 LOOKING SOUTHWEST

EAST LOCUST STREET AT FIRST STREET JULY 6, 1911 LOOKING NORTHWEST

Infrastructure projects that had been delayed through bureaucracy were moved to the forefront after the reorganization of the Des Moines city government in 1907. Along with the establishment of a civic center along the riverfront, one of the main priorities was paving the streets. These before and after photographs, printed in the *Des Moines Annual Report* in 1913, show the progress made by the Public Works Department in just two years. (From *Des Moines Annual Report.*)

The temperance movement had a strong voice in Iowa, with several attempts to make Iowa a dry state in the late 1800s. After the repeal of Prohibition, a moderate consensus was reached to allow the sale of alcohol but regulate its use. This bar near the capitol was eventually torn down through urban renewal projects in the 1970s, and the State Historical Society of Iowa built its new museum and library on the block in 1987. (Courtesy Library of Congress.)

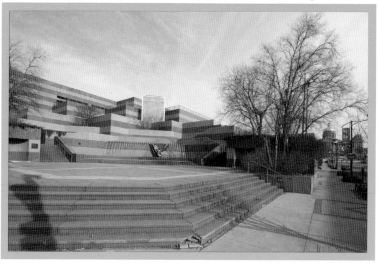

James D. Edbundson sponsored the arts in Des Moines with a bequest after his death in 1933. The Des Moines Art Center is located in Greenwood Park at 4700 Grand Avenue. The first wing was designed by architect Eliel Saarinen and opened in 1948; a second wing was opened in 1968, designed by I.M. Pei, along with a third expansion by Richard Meier in 1985. Another bequest by John and Mary Pappajohn allowed the creation of the sculpture park at 1330 Grand Avenue. Both the museum and park are open to the public free of charge. (Courtesy Ron Playle.)

This view down Locust Street from Ninth Street shows another perspective of the Equitable Building. The structure on the right is the former Des Moines Club, which provided a members-only place to relax for businessmen in the downtown area. When the club relocated to the Ruan Center, the building served as the meeting place for the Za-Ga-Zig Shriners Temple before being converted to luxury suites. (Courtesy Ron Playle.)

This Mobil station was located on the corner of Locust and Fourth Streets, the old site of the Observatory Building. Looking north, many smaller businesses line the downtown streets during that time. After a careful look at the end of the road, a Buick dealership is visible where Domino's Pizza is now. If the parking garage were not in the way, it would be possible to see Wells Fargo Arena and the Iowa Events Center. (Courtesy Des Moines Public Library.)

This view of the Des Moines riverfront looking north shows the many bridges crossing the river. The rail yards were still quite busy in the 1940s, with passenger and cargo service provided by the Rock Island, Milwaukee, and Chicago Great Western railroads. One trestle remains an active line; the remaining bridges have been torn down or converted to pedestrian use as part of the Principal Riverwalk. Center Street Bridge is in the distance with dual paths for bicyclists and joggers. (Courtesy the author.)

This view down Locust Street from the capitol steps shows the significant changes in the skyline over the years. Perhaps a more interesting difference, though, is the replacement of the parking lot in front of the Iowa State Capitol with an extensive 10-acre terrace, with memorial gardens lining the walkway on both sides. Final construction on the project was completed in 2010. (Courtesy Ron Playle.)

This view of downtown facing south down Fifth Avenue shows the twin WHO radio masts atop the Liberty Building, then the headquarters of Banker's Life (now Principal Financial Group). Banker's Life actually owned the radio station for many years. The broadcast trucks parked in front of the Polk County Convention Center in the Now image are covering the 2012 Iowa Caucuses. (Courtesy Des Moines Public Library.)

THE JOURNEY TO NOW

5 Locust Looking East   Register & Tribune Bldg, Des Moines, Iowa

The Register and Tribune Building is the home of the *Des Moines Register*. The original *Register* newspaper, on Court Avenue, merged with the *Leader* in 1903, combining the two largest morning papers in the city. This was followed by the purchase of the *Evening Tribune* in 1908. After this merger, only two other papers competed with the *Register*—the *Daily Capital* and the *Daily News*. By 1927, these two papers were absorbed as well. The *Tribune* ceased publication in 1982. The building's gray stone facade was replaced with a Modernist curtain wall in the 1970s. (Courtesy Ron Playle.)

The Reverend George Peak was the president of the Central Life Association Society of the U.S., now known as AmerUs. He built this Colonial Revival home at 1080 Twenty-second Street in 1900. In a major renovation, the large porch was removed. Listed in the National Register of Historic Places in 1978 as the New Life Eternity House, it now serves as a center of ministry for interfaith renewal. (Courtesy Des Moines Public Library.)

George Reynolds, the president of Des Moines National Bank, lived in this house at 1623 Center Street, in the Sherman Hill district. Built in 1882 in the Italianate style, it is listed in the National Register of Historic Places as the Maish House and remains a private residence today. The Sherman Hill Association continues to look for opportunities to preserve old homes by relocating them to the district. (From *Des Moines Illustrated Souvenir*.)

Oak Park was one of the many neighborhoods developed as Des Moines expanded to the north. This home at 1408 Douglas Avenue, built in 1910, was the residence of the Magee family by 1921, when this photograph was taken. The home was expanded and refurbished in the 1970s and remains a private residence today. (Courtesy Des Moines Public Library.)

THE JOURNEY TO NOW

George France, a philanthropist with businesses in lending and real estate, built this house in the River Bend area at the corner of Oakland and Franklin Avenues in the early 1900s. The property was later subdivided and the house converted to apartments in the 1940s. Though the neighborhood has seen urban decay, recent revitalization efforts have brought the luster back to many of the homes in the area. (From *Des Moines Beautiful.*)

The Des Moines Auditorium, built in 1908 on Fourth Street north of Grand Avenue, was a popular place for plays, town meetings, debates, and an occasional revival preacher. Though the building still stands today, it is hardly recognizable as originally constructed. It was extensively remodeled to serve as a Buick dealership and eventually became a garage. (From *Des Moines Beautiful*.)

Hoyt Sherman was probably the most recognizable early pioneer of Des Moines. Brother of Civil War general William T. Sherman, he served as postmaster and was a real estate developer and cofounder of several businesses. He built this home at Fifteenth Street and Woodland Avenue in the Sherman Hill area in 1877. Upon his death, this home and his extensive art collection were donated to the Des Moines Women's Club. In 1922, a theater was added, which hosts many plays and speakers to this day. (Courtesy Ron Playle.)

In this view of Seventh Street facing north from Walnut Street, many retail establishments available to residents in the 1950s are shown. Specialty shops, dry goods, and general stores had always been a part of downtown Des Moines. In the 1920s, however, these small shops began taking a backseat to large department stores such as Younker Brothers and Harris-Emery. National chains, such as Sears, Roebuck and Co.; J.C. Penney; and S.S. Kresge—the forerunner of Kmart—also began to move in. (Courtesy Iowa Department of Transportation.)

The city center was vibrant with life, as seen in this view of Walnut Street facing east from Seventh Street. But in the 1960s, suburban malls began to take over, and most of the retail stores moved out. Now, Walnut Street is a transit mall, exclusively for bus traffic during the day. There have been proposals to revitalize retail downtown by converting Walnut Street back to two-way traffic, while still leaving room for outdoor cafés and other venues. (Courtesy Iowa Department of Transportation.)

By the 1950s, cars had taken over trolley and most bus service in Des Moines, as can be seen in this view taken from the municipal building between the Locust Street and Grand Avenue bridges. The tallest structure in this view is actually the WHO radio mast, though the new Equitable Building overshadows many of the other high-rises in the downtown area. The Simon Estes Amphitheater on the riverfront now features concerts during the summer months. (Courtesy Des Moines Public Library.)

THE JOURNEY TO NOW

This view down Locust Street includes the first parking garages in the city, just in front of the Equitable Building on the right. These garages first started appearing in 1950, with the Mulberry Street Garage and the Fourth Street and Locust Elevator Garage, both of which have since been torn down. (Courtesy the author.)

In this scene, an electric bus picks up travelers on the corner of Sixth Avenue and Locust Street. Des Moines has a long history with mass transit; the city began electric trolley service in 1888, becoming only the second city in America to offer it. By the 1950s, however, the trolley rails were removed, and electric buses took their place. Now, Des Moines Area Regional Transit (DART) runs diesel buses almost exclusively. There is some discussion of bringing back the trolleys, but it would cost millions of dollars to do so. (Courtesy Iowa Department of Transportation.)

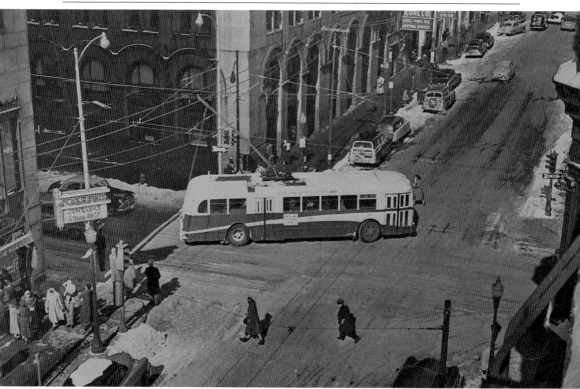

East Fourteenth Street (US Highway 69) was one of the first highways established during the early days of the automobile, providing access to Ames and points north. It was extended southward toward Indianola in the 1930s and became one of the main avenues of growth for the city during the war years. Southridge Mall was built in 1970s, and the highway continues to attract retail and commercial space to the south side of Des Moines. (Courtesy Iowa Department of Transportation.)

Central Life began the construction of its new headquarters in 1953 at Fifth Avenue and Keo Way (now Watson Powell Jr. Parkway). The company was later bought by AmerUS, then sold to Aviva, which continues to use the facility. Insurance and financial services have always been a solid part of the business landscape, with insurance providers such as Travelers, Principal, Nationwide, Equitable (now part of ING), and Dial Financial (later a subsidiary of Wells Fargo) established in Des Moines. (Courtesy Des Moines Public Library.)

This view of the Roosevelt Center from 1950 demonstrates the early evolution of retail away from business districts downtown to shopping centers closer to residential areas. Located on Forty-second Street north of I-235, it continues to attract business, but many other shopping centers and malls in the area have large numbers of vacancies, as retail venues try to compete with big-box stores. (Courtesy Des Moines Public Library.)

The neighborhood around Drake University developed its own regional business district at Twenty-fourth Street and University Avenue as residents moved into the area. In this view facing west, just beyond the storefronts is the First Christian Church on the left, with the Drake campus across the street to the right. Though the district itself is thriving, very few of the buildings survived from the 1950s to today. (Courtesy Iowa Department of Transportation.)

This view shows University Avenue facing east from Twenty-fifth Street. In the 1960s and 1970s, many old homes in the Drake area were subdivided into apartments as the entire area declined. The Drake Neighborhood Association fought to change that trend, starting in 1979. It worked to identify homes of historical interest and get them registered and restored. The neighborhood continues to be one of the most interesting and diverse in the state. (Courtesy Iowa Department of Transportation.)

After construction of Interstates 80 and 35 was completed west of the city in 1958, construction began on the Interstate 235 corridor, including this bridge across the Des Moines River. Many older neighborhoods and historic civic buildings were condemned. To alleviate concerns about destroying historic buildings, an urban renewal plan was included in the project, which dedicated land on both sides of the freeway to new commercial development. (Courtesy Iowa Department of Transportation.)

THE JOURNEY TO NOW

The northern section of Interstate 35 to Ames was completed in 1965, seen here on opening day in this view looking south towards the eastern "mixmaster," where Interstates 80, 35, and 235 meet. The final leg of 235 would not be completed until 1968. As many expected, urban decay set in as people migrated along the paths of the freeway to the suburbs, and urban renewal projects in the 1980s proposed solutions to the problems. (Courtesy Iowa Department of Transportation.)

Valley Junction was founded in 1893 to support the Rock Island rail yards. When they moved out, the city voted to rename itself West Des Moines. It has had a varied history, from small town to suburb because of the building of the freeways. New developments, such as Jordan Creek and West Glen, and new business expansions like Wells Fargo have made the city a financial center in its own right. The old downtown area still serves as a haven for antique collectors. (Courtesy Des Moines Public Library.)

Merle Hay Plaza, built on the site of St. Gabriel's Monastery, was the first—and for a time the largest—mall in the state. Straddling the border of Des Moines and Urbandale, it was enclosed in 1972 and expanded to double its size two years later. Once they began visiting malls, many residents never went downtown to shop again, and many of the larger department stores moved to the suburbs. (Courtesy the author.)

By 1981, city planners realized they had to do something and established several urban renewal projects for the downtown area. One of the key proposals was to find ways to bring people back to the city center. Plaza Condominiums was one of the first residential developments designed to do just that. Built in 1985, it continues to offer upscale living with convenient access to offices, retailers, and events in the downtown area. (Courtesy Des Moines Public Library.)

Another question was how to attract more retail space to downtown. The Hub Tower, also built in 1985 with mixed-use facilities, offered a way to do that through the Kaleidoscope Mall on the first three stories of the building. Although it did succeed in bringing in retail options, it has met with mixed success, especially since Younkers Department Store across the street closed its doors. (Courtesy Des Moines Public Library.)

An important aspect of downtown's renewal was the skywalk system, which connected most of the downtown buildings together above street level in climate-controlled conditions. Although it has also helped retail establishments along the skywalk, most of the downtown population leaves after 5:00 p.m., and the system is virtually deserted on the weekends. Street-level vendors have also complained about the loss of foot traffic they have experienced. (Courtesy Des Moines Public Library.)

Capital Square, Nollen Plaza, and the Iowa Events Center were the first in a multitude of projects helping to breathe life back into downtown. Renewal has continued through condominium projects, new office space such as the Principal headquarters at 801 Grand Avenue, and beautification efforts like the Western Gateway Park, the Principal Riverwalk, and the new Science Center and development along Court Avenue. (Courtesy Des Moines Public Library.)

One of the most recent efforts was the retrofit and recladding of the Neal Smith Federal Building. Built in 1964, it suffered from leaky roofs, cracking masonry, and a generally unappealing layout. Another primary goal was the installation of energy-efficient technologies. The project was performed in several phases, with the last being completed in 2011. (Courtesy Des Moines Public Library.)

Comparing the city skyline from what it looked like even 10 years ago shows how much the community continues to improve. The completion of the Martin Luther King Jr. Parkway Bridge is just the next step in extending the road to the US Highway 65 bypass. Although there have been times of struggle, such as the floods of 1993 and the impact of the financial crisis, the people of Des Moines have continued to find ways to make this city one of the top places to live and work. (Courtesy Iowa Tourism Office.)

Discover Thousands of Local History Books Featuring Millions of Vintage Images

Arcadia Publishing, the leading local history publisher in the United States, is committed to making history accessible and meaningful through publishing books that celebrate and preserve the heritage of America's people and places.

Find more books like this at
www.arcadiapublishing.com

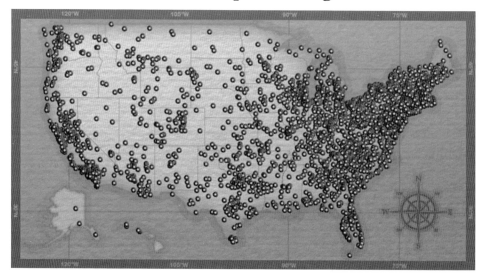

Search for your hometown history, your old stomping grounds, and even your favorite sports team.

Consistent with our mission to preserve history on a local level, this book was printed in South Carolina on American-made paper and manufactured entirely in the United States. Products carrying the accredited Forest Stewardship Council (FSC) label are printed on 100 percent FSC-certified paper.

MADE IN THE